Indoor Succulent Care

A Beginner's Guide on How Succulent Plants Can Keep You Out of Trouble and Make You a Better Person

By Succulent Circle

Copyright © 2020

All rights reserved. No part of this book may be reproduced or used in any manner without the written consent of the copyright owner except for the use of quotations in a book review.

www.succulentcircle.com

Table of Contents

Introduction	5
Chapter 1 - Identifying Your Succulents	6
Chapter 2 - Tips for Growing Succulents	10
Chapter 3 - How to Water Succulent Plants	15
Chapter 4 - Tips for Planting Succulents in Containers	18
Chapter 5 - How to Prevent Succulent from Dying	21
Chapter 6 - How to Get Rid of Bugs on Succulents	25
Chapter 7 - What to Do with Succulents Growing Tall	27
Chapter 8 - Propagate Succulents from Leaves and Cuttings	31
Conclusion	34

Introduction

Bringing a succulent home is a very exciting time in your life. And we're to make it enjoyable and help keep your succulent healthy.

The information in this guide can help you make the best choices when taking care of your plant. Please ponder over it carefully and practice the methods suggested.

Much of the methods mentioned in the book can be applied to all of the indoor succulents available in the world. While weather conditions and geo-environments demand that we adjust our methods now and then, the basic practices remain the same.

The information presented represents a combination of our personal experience and of those who are masters in this area. May the wealth of information presented here benefit you and your succulent for years to come.

Chapter 1 - Identifying Your Succulents

For those overwhelmed by the pace of this busy modern life, plants can provide a mindful and a break from the constant rush. Think about the beautiful plants and trees you enjoy looking at. Aren't they beautiful?

Sometimes you may think that gardening or farming is something out of the way for us due to the time that needs to be invested.

But, if you are thinking about raising or buying succulents, then nothing can be more enjoyable.

Let's dive into on how we can identify our succulents.

Knowing the Type of your Succulent Plant

Identifying your succulents can be mind-boggling, especially since they come in numerous types.

There are over 30 plant families, with each having multiple plant species within them.

A fun fact associated with succulents is that while many species look completely different from each other, some of them are wildly similar. A wrong identification may lead to a dead succulent or a sick family member.

Adding to this dilemma is the fact that many nurseries who sell them don't label them accurately, or don't label them at all. Hence trying to identify your plants can be a challenge in patience. But, there are different ways in which this can be achieved.

Study Your Succulent

Succulents have an excellent ability to store water in their leaves, stems, and roots. This feature not only allows them to thrive in harsh habitation, but also gives them a distinctive appearance.

Some succulents have unusual and abnormal growth forms and shapes. If you have an unidentified succulent, then the first step is to study the characteristics of the plant.

Remember, the most important parts of any succulent are its color, leaves, flower, spikes, and overall size.

However, succulents have a distinctive feature in one of the above characteristics which separate them from other species of the same family.

Once you have studied the above parts carefully, determine their characteristics in terms of shape, size, and thickness.

Studying the above characteristics not only allows us to take care of them, but also know its name. Once you are fairly aware of your plant, you will need to move on to the next important step.

Take a Photo of Your Succulent

After studying the characteristics in detail, take a picture of your succulent in clear light. You must take photos of all the different parts of your plant so that all details are visible.

While taking the photo, use a subtle background, so that the clarity of your plant doesn't get distorted. It's best to have a light-colored background which does not disturb the composition of the image. Also, avoid those parts of the plants which have holes, scratches or dead leaves as this will leave the image cluttered, and angle yourself in a way that the shadows don't fall in your plant.

The power of a beautiful image cannot be underestimated. A good photo not only helps you identify the plant but also increases the beauty of your flower. You can share the photo with others too. Hence, if you have access to good cameras or a photographer, go ahead and experiment with a few ideas. You will not be disappointed with the results.

Once you have a good quality image, you will now need to use some research methods.

Comprehensive Research

Do extensive research on authoritative websites to understand the characteristics of your plant. It's important to find details about your plants such as its color, length, if it has any flowers, and whether its leaves have any spikes or thorns.

Succulents have a distinctive appearance and hence finding information about them is easy.

If you don't get adequate information from the web, the best option is to contact succulent experts and have a chat with them to get a greater insight into your plant.

Also, share the photo to like-minded succulent lovers who may help you in identifying it.

You can use social media and ask your social media friends to help you identify your succulents.

Once your plant is accurately identified, study all the details about it. Don't forget to return the favor and help others who may be looking for help for their succulents.

Chapter 2 - Tips for Growing Succulents

Succulents are by nature very forgiving and easy to grow plants. They have easily transitioned from the deserts and arid regions to our homes and offices. In fact, you can design your own indoor garden using succulents as they can easily hang from a ceiling hook and can also grow from a dim corner of your home.

If you are planning to grow your own succulent, then you have the option to either grow them from seeds, leaves, stems, or trimmings. No matter whether you purchase or decide to grow, the following tips are extremely necessary to get healthy plants:

Planting Your Succulent

If you have purchased a succulent and are planting it into your own pot, then make sure to use the same soil composition that was used by the seller.

Try to keep the same atmosphere as the plant was exposed; if not, then slowly acclimatize the plant to your surroundings after a few days.

Once you have decided where to plant your succulent, the step is to prepare the soil.

Soil

Succulents are known for growing in any type of environment. However, your main concern should not be just to plant the succulent, but to have an environment where it will thrive.

The secret for healthy succulents is two parts of well-drained soil with one part of drainage material.

The more your soil remains wet, the more damage it will cause.

As a caution, if you use regular garden soil, the succulent may rot away.

Watering Your Plants

Succulents thrive in low-water conditions as their leaves and stems absorb and store water. Hence, your succulent will need less water. The main idea is to let the soil remain dry between 2 sessions of watering.

Depending upon your plant, if you decide to water once or twice a week, then let the soil dry completely before watering again.

Also, while watering them during the growing stage, use a spray bottle and *spray water directly on the soil* and not on the plant.

If you let your succulent go without water for weeks, then they may not die, but may stop growing.

Generally speaking, water them at least once a week.

Using Fertilizers

It is advisable to use water-soluble fertilizer once a year (maybe late summer) to give the additional nutrient boost.

The best way to is to take half a dose of well-balanced organic fertilizer and put it on the soil during the time plants enter their growing season (spring).

Direction of Sunlight

Succulents need less direct sunlight and hence can thrive even indoors.

The best place to put your plant would be in a shady place where it gets a small level of indirect sunlight.

Some people hang their plants in their balcony, while some keep it on their working table.

It is advisable to keep your plant on a south-facing window for at least 6 hours a day.

If you keep your plant in direct sunlight, the leaves may start rotting, and if you keep it in a dark corner, the stems may reach out for light, thus growing in an abnormal direction. You may find it difficult to keep them growing straight.

Let's understand the different ways of growing your succulents

Growing Succulents From Seeds

Growing succulents from seeds may be a tricky job as the seeds look like fine dust and it may become difficult to identify if they are genuine.

The foremost thing to remember is to buy good quality seeds from a reputable seller. Many sellers have a large variety of seeds and you may have to do thorough research on the type of succulent you want to raise to be sure about its care and maintenance.

As a caution, many sellers sell cultivated varieties of seeds, or hybrid seeds, which may not give the ideal result. Even though the plant may grow, it may not be the same plant that you wanted!

Also, some succulents may take weeks to germinate, hence carefully select your plant seed after researching about its rate of growth.

Growing Succulents From Leaves

The best way to grow succulents is to grow them from leaves and cuttings.

Most succulents grow from fallen leaves.

The biggest advantage of growing succulents from leaves is that you can predict how your plant will look, which is not possible with seeds.

Chapter 3 - How to Water Succulent Plants

As we mentioned in the previous chapter, succulents don't need much water.

They have the exceptional ability to store water in their leaves and stem, but that doesn't absolve you of the responsibility of watering them.

The most important thing to remember is that *you want your succulents to thrive*, not just survive!

These are plants that need a delicate balance between over-watering and under-watering. The following points will help you to achieve that delicate balance.

Check the Soil Thoroughly Before Watering

The condition of your soil is extremely important for the root system of your plant. One fact that you always need to remember is that the soil should never be wet or moist before watering.

If you look at your plant and you see that the soil is not completely dry, then it is best to wait for another day.

To check the soil, put your finger an inch into the soil. If wet soil is stuck on your finger, then watering can wait.

Soak the Soil

If you have noticed that the soil is dry and needs to be watered, then pour water into the soil till it soaks completely and runs down the drainage hole of your pot.

The water needs to run down the soil completely, because if it stays on the surface, the roots or the stem may start to rot. The water that settles in the plate should be cleaned so that it doesn't disturb the base soil.

Many succulents grow slowly between late fall to early spring (during winters) and hence you can increase the intervals between your watering.

Research about your plant to see their periods of dormancy and growth.

Check the Condition of Your Plant

If you notice that your plant leaves are getting fluffy or discolored even after regular watering, then it's time to assess your watering habits.

If your soil is well-drained, then you may need to revise the frequency of watering. If the problem persists, then you may need to check the soil and the aggregates in it.

If you have the resources to collect rainwater, then they are the best for your plants! Tap water contains minerals that may cause long term harm to your plant.

Remember, we need to water the plants only when the soil is completely dry.

If the soil takes 5 days to dry, then water every 5 days. If the soil dries after 8 days, then water every 8 days.

Chapter 4 - Tips for Planting Succulents in Containers

Succulents add beauty to your home with its decorative flowers and leaves.

They grow in any type of pots, but it's best to buy indoor containers for adding that additional level of creativity to your indoor garden.

The following steps will ensure your indoor container garden looks beautiful at its best!

Choosing the Right Container

Succulents need less water, but a good home to thrive in.

Choose a container that is shallow, wide and has ample drainage at the bottom.

The size of the pot should be big enough for the roots to spread out. A dish-sized container would work well.

Use a tray, plate, or a small screening to cover the base of the container so that the soil stays in the container while the water is draining.

It is always best for the container to be 4-5 inches deep and twice the diameter of its nursery pot.

Preparing the Soil in Your Container

Since the succulents would be in your nursery pot, you will have to successfully transfer them into your pot.

Put the right mix of soil and gravel into your container, around one quarter below its surface.

After putting the soil, design a mental outline of where you will plant your succulents if you have more than one.

Transferring Your Plant

Carefully remove your plant from the nursery pot without damaging its leaves and roots.

Don't pull by the leaves, but gently massage the soil to remove the plant. Then place your plant in your container by adjusting it well into the soil. Fill the spaces with some more soil.

Always ensure that your succulent is not too deep inside the pot to avoid water-logging in the bowl. Once the plant is fit into the soil, take additional soil and fill in the container to ensure that your plant is well- rooted.

Decorate your container by planting multiple succulents in one container.

Plant the biggest plant in the center and the smaller ones surrounding it.

Plants that are close to each other will grow slowly while those with spaces between them will grow faster.

Clean Your Container

Once your plants are solidly fixed, use a light brush to clean your container and your plants. Brush off the soil from the leaves and stems. To add to the beauty of your plant, top the container with smooth stones or gravel of different sizes and colors.

It is important that the soil should not touch the crown of the plant, neither should spaces be left on the soil surface or else the roots will rot. If rotten roots are left untreated, the plants will start dying.

Chapter 5 - How to Prevent Succulent from Dying

When it comes to taking care of our succulents, there are so many things you can work on.

We can'y neglect our succulents and expect them to thrive. That's why you need some strategies and support to prevent your succulent from dying.

First and foremost tip – Treat your plant as a family and inspect it every day. Nothing can be better than to find time for your plant. Set-up some helpful reminders to help you check on your plants regularly.

If you inspect the plants regularly, you will find that your succulents will be automated, and will need much less attention from you.

Now that you are following this important step, you'll have to follow some more simple steps to ensure your plants are always healthy and you don't suffer from soggy stems, discolored and fluffy leaves.

Keep Checking the Soil

The roots of your succulent plants need a rapid exchange of water and air to survive.

This means the roots will thrive only if the soil is dry and the water passes through the soil quickly. If you notice that the soil in your container or pot remains wet for a long time, then it means that your soil mix is not letting the water drain down.

In such cases, you may have to re-pot your succulent.

For a new pot, prepare an appropriate mix of potting soil, perlite, gravel, or crushed sand and mix them well.

The soil should be crumbly and porous and should not form a lump. If you ensure that your soil is porous, your plant roots will remain healthy.

Re-pot your succulents every couple of years. Don't add any organic material to your soil.

Wait Before you Water

Water for succulents is what dessert is for us. You take them in small quantities.

Succulents don't like drowning in water, make sure that water them only when it's absolutely necessary – sometimes once a week. Watering them often is one of the primary reasons why people lose their succulents.

Before watering your succulent, ensure, and we repeat, ensure that the soil is completely dry and crumbly. If you decide that it's time to water, don't put smaller shots of water.

Pour water in the pot continuously till it pours down the drainage hole and then stops. Such deeper watering ensures that the entire soil in your pot is drenched at once and gets dry at one.

If you pour water in smaller shots, then only the top few inches will get watered and the water may not pour down, leading to root rot and eventual death.

Pour water into the soil and not over your leaves, for this may lead to the growth of fungus on them.

Shallow Pots

Succulent plants are fond of *shallow pots* where the roots get enough water before they drain. If the pot is deep, water may drain down the pot quickly before soaking the roots.

Location of Your Plants

While succulents are indoor plants, it doesn't mean that they can survive just any environment. Your plant may die, if it is near a cooling vent, or it stays in an air-conditioned room.

If you have a balcony, you can keep it there, or you can keep it inside your house at a place where it can get adequate, if not direct sunlight.

Don't overcrowd your pot with many plants. Keep your pot by the window where the sunlight is not the strongest.

The best way to save any succulent is to research well about your plant and check what conditions are the best for it.

Chapter 6 - How to Get Rid of Bugs on Succulents

Insects can be a real annoyance for your succulents. These bugs are so tiny that you may not even notice them feeding on the leaves, stem and even the roots of your healthy plants. Left untreated, they can cause serious damage beyond your control.

Since these small bugs can spread to your other succulents, some simple measures should be taken to ensure that your succulents remain bug- free.

If the Bugs Are Tiny White Mealybugs

These bugs are gray-colored bugs that almost look like dirt. If you have rubbing alcohol, dip a cotton swab in it and gently apply it to the area which is infested by bugs.

Sometimes, bugs may be in areas where they are not visible, so to be extra cautious as to not injure the plant, put water into the alcohol and dilute it and spray it on that area.

If you notice that the bugs have spread to the roots, then gently remove the plant and treat the roots in the same way.

Repeat this treatment every week until the bugs are cleared.

If the problem persists for a long time, pour alcohol into the soil which will kill the bugs or insects hidden into the soil.

While treating your succulent, its best to isolate it from other plants.

Also, instead of using alcohol, some have found that using soap water also works better.

If the Bugs Are Larger

Some bugs like gnats may damage the plant more than you have expected.

Some insects are also responsible for causing scales and brown spots on the plants.

Gnats look like small mosquitoes and get attracted to your succulent due to moisture present on it.

If your plant is developing such scales, it is best to scrape them off the plant before spraying alcohol on them.

To ensure that gnats stay away, keep the plant and the soil dry and check that your drainage hole is perfect for your pot.

Sometimes putting cinnamon powder on the base of your soil will ensure that it does not attract insects or fungus.

If the problem with bugs persists even after all treatments, consider re-potting your plant in different soil mix and use insect pads to curb the issue.

Chapter 7 - What to Do with Succulents Growing Tall

The main reason why people love succulents is their small size and beautiful structure.

However, if your succulent starts stretching out, or is growing tall, then you may need to take a few measures to ensure they remain beautiful and not abnormal.

If you don't take active steps now, your succulents won't just grow tall, but its stems may get intertwined leading to a ghastly sight!

Why Are They Growing Tall?

As a succulent lover, one basic thing to remember is – if your succulent is stretching out, then it's not getting adequate sunlight.

So, the best way to nurture your plant is to keep it near sunlight, if not in direct sunlight.

Sometimes, the reason for the growth may not be sunlight, but the nature of the plant. Some succulent plants grow tall naturally, so it is wise to keep pruning them regularly. The best way is to give way the cuttings so that others may propagate them and start their succulent garden.

How to Cut the Plant Stems and Leaves

If you have decided to prune your plant, use clean and sharp scissors or pruners to cut the plants.

Rusted pruners may infect the plant, which may cause more damage.

While pruning, make sure that the plant has enough healthy leaves to photosynthesize.

How to Prevent them from Growing Again

To prevent them from growing tall, apart from pruning you may also need to re-pot the plant and place the container/pot near sunlight.

If that's not possible, you can keep your plant near sunlight for a few hours every day.

When your succulents grow tall, the leaves may discolor and may attract bugs.

The best thing in this is that unlike other plants, you have the possibility of propagating your cuttings, so in a sense, you are not killing your plant, but giving them a new beginning!

Choosing the Right Pot for Your Succulents

Your succulents need an ideal home to grow, live, and thrive.

While some planters choose a pot for increasing the beauty of their plant, but the right kind of pot means life for your succulent.

Pot's come in various materials and each has its advantages and disadvantages. Some individuals select plastic containers due to their affordability. While these may seem easy to carry, it holds moisture longer and may prove harmful in the long run.

On the other hand, wooden pots are aesthetic and remain cool during sunny days, however, they are prone to rot.

Metal pots are not recommended as they rust easily and absorb heat which can burn the plant. Fiberglass can discolor and flake easily.

If you live in a cool-weather area, then ceramic or terracotta plants are the right choice. These materials increase airflow and fight the problem of over-watering.

Terra-cotta pots dry quickly and are very easy to work with. Also, to add beauty to your garden, you can also use wall hanging baskets (with proper drainage hole) for hanging your succulents.

The material of the pot depends a lot on the weather of your location, so choose a pot after thorough research and study.

Size of the Pot

The roots of your plant can get sorely affected by the size of your pot.

If your pot is very small, the plant may not get enough nutrients, thus disturbing its growth.

On the other hand, larger pots hold more water, and the trapped moisture can damage the roots of the plants.

Many succulent lovers suggest that the container of your pot should be 10% larger than the diameter of the width of your succulent.

Hence, smaller succulents will require a smaller container with barely one or two inches of empty space around it.

If you have a bigger container, then you can choose to grow multiple plants to offset the size factor.

If you still decide the use a larger pot, then fill the bottom few inches with gravel, or stones so that water drains down fast.

In the end, no matter what type of pot you select, always keep a decent- sized drainage hole at the bottom.

Chapter 8 - Propagate Succulents from Leaves and Cuttings

Succulent is one of a kind plant where it is easier to grow them from existing plants, than raising them from seeds.

If you have plants that have overgrown or if your friend gives you some of his succulent cuttings, then you can grow your new plants.

The best time to propagate a succulent is during the beginning of the spring months when they in their most active growth phase.

Succulents propagated at this time have better chances for survival.

Removing Leaves From Your Succulent

First and foremost, if you are removing the leaves from your succulent, then remember that the way you remove it will affect on whether your plant will grow or not.

For a successful propagation, choose a leaf that is fresh, plump, and fluffy. Such leaves are easier to pull from the stem.

While pulling the leaf, ensure your hands are clean, and that you twist it completely from the stem.

If the leaf breaks in between, it will die, as the base of the leaf is important for propagation.

If twisting is not possible, gently wiggle the leaf both sides and eventually, it will come off.

If at all you decide to use a knife, then use a sterile one and cleanly cut it at the base ensuring that no part is left on the stem.

After the leaf is removed, put it on a paper towel to heal or dry for 2 to 3 days.

If you plant the leaf before healing it, it will absorb too much water when you water it for the first time.

Planting the Leaves

The leaves should not be pressed into the soil.

Rather lay it on top of the succulent soil mix and put the pot in bright sunlight. The succulent is at the stage where it needs more water and sunlight.

Hence water them a few times a week. Use a spray bottle to spray water on the leaves and soil rather than drenching them completely.

After a few weeks, you will see small plant shoots coming off the leaf. Once the original leaf has dried up, it means that the plant is now ready for re-potting.

Carefully pick the new plant and plant it into a new container.

During the growing stage of these new plants, the roots need soil, hence ensure that the roots are covered with soil completely. Succulent propagation has a low success rate, hence use multiple leaves while propagating.

Propagating from Cuttings

Many succulents grow best from stem cuttings, as these have stronger stems and smaller leaves.

Propagating plants from stems is comparatively easy than from leaves as it doesn't need to be put on the soil, but can be directly potted in soil.

Choose a stem that is young and growing and cut it with a sharp knife close to its base of the parent stem. Like leaves, the stem should be cut- off from its base and then left to dry for 4 weeks on a paper towel.

After it dries, re-pot it into a new pot and keeps it in sunlight and water a few times a week to let it grow.

After a few weeks, baby stems will grow around it, giving you a beautiful new beginning to a new generation of succulents.

Conclusion

To raise succulents means to start the journey with the end in mind. It means that you should know all the different ways to take care of your plant and ensure that you are taking the necessary steps in the right direction.

When responsibilities increase and stresses come in our life, we tend to revert to nature for gaining a measure of serenity. Having plants in our home gives us the necessary balance, and increases our emotional stability.

Their beauty enamors us and reminds us that sometimes it is necessary to take a break from life.

May this guide help you in carving your house garden and may your plants fill your house with colors and your life with joy.

Visit us at our website to receive

educational information on Succulent Care.

www.SucculentCircle.com

Printed in Great Britain
by Amazon